OVERCOMING BARRIERS

What Is It Like to Be Blind?

Deborah Kent

Enslow Elementary
an imprint of
Enslow Publishers, Inc.
40 Industrial Road
Box 398
Berkeley Heights, NJ 07922
USA

http://www.enslow.com

Enslow Elementary, an imprint of Enslow Publishers, Inc.

Enslow Elementary® is a registered trademark of Enslow Publishers, Inc.

Copyright © 2012 by Enslow Publishers, Inc.

Library of Congress Cataloging-in-Publication Data

    Kent, Deborah.
     What is it like to be blind? / Deborah Kent.
       p. cm. — (Overcoming barriers)
     Includes bibliographical references and index.
     Summary: "Follows the everyday lives of several blind school children, describing how they use Braille to read,
how they use their other senses to navigate their environment, what they do for fun, and how being blind does not
stop them from pursuing their dreams"—Provided by publisher.
     ISBN 978-0-7660-3768-7
     1. Blind children—Juvenile literature. I. Title.
     HV1596.3.K46 2012
     305.9'081—dc22
                2010045200

Future editions:
Paperback ISBN 978-1-4644-0153-4
ePUB ISBN 978-1-4645-1060-1
PDF ISBN 978-1-4646-1060-8

Printed in China

012012 Leo Paper Group, Heshan City, Guangdong, China

10 9 8 7 6 5 4 3 2 1

Photo Credits: © 2011 Photos.com, a division of Getty Images, p. 32; © Abramorama/Courtesy Everett
Collection, p. 37; AP Images: Ajit Solanki, p. 22, Carlos Osorio, p. 13, Don Petersen, p. 12, The Daily News,
Hillary Wundrow, p. 18, The Herald, Dan Bates, p. 8, Idaho State Journal, Bill Schaefer, p. 29, The Vicksburg
Post, Katie Carter, p. 30; Courtesy of the Chamberlain family, pp. 24, 27, 33; Courtesy of Nelly and
Everardo Gamino, pp. 17, 21; Courtesy of Sally Thomas, pp. 35, 38; Courtesy of Zina Lewis, pp. 4, 7, 43;
© Jonathan Nourok/PhotoEdit, p. 39; Press Association via AP Images, p. 10; © Robin Sachs/PhotoEdit, p. 20;
Shutterstock.com, pp. 1, 19, 25; WAN XIANG/Xinhua/Landov, p. 15.

Cover Photo: © Myrleen Ferguson Cate/PhotoEdit

Contents

MarChé Daughtry loves to do everything that other teenagers do—shop, listen to music, and think about her future.

Chapter 1

A Touch of Fame

When she was in fifth grade, MarChé Daughtry was on TV. She had won a prize in a contest for children who read Braille. MarChé read aloud on camera from a Braille book. She showed how she used a computer that spoke the words on the screen. The reporter explained that MarChé had earned straight A's three years in a row. MarChé hoped that her story would show people that blind children can be successful when they go to regular schools.

Today MarChé is thirteen and in eighth grade. She lives in Virginia. She is interested in all animals, especially pandas and black leopards. She enjoys listening to music and shopping for clothes. When she goes out she uses her long white cane. The cane warns her of steps, poles, and other things in her path.

MarChé loves to read. She has enough sight to read print when the letters are very large. However, she finds reading Braille much faster and easier. Her favorite books are novels in the Harry Potter and Twilight series.

Read by Touch

Braille is a method of reading by touch. It is used by blind people all over the world. The Braille code is made up of patterns of dots that form letters, numbers, and punctuation marks. Blind people read by moving their fingers lightly across the Braille lines.

MarChé uses her white cane to check the ground around her when she goes out. This way she does not trip over things.

Books in Braille have raised dots for letters and punctuation. It is easy to use your fingers to feel the bumps and read the book if you know the Braille code.

Chapter 2

The World by Sound and Touch

If you can see, you probably think it would be very scary to be blind. Maybe you've tried wearing a blindfold or walking around with your eyes closed. You were afraid of tripping or bumping into things. You imagine that being blind must be like living in the dark all the time.

However, blindness is not frightening to a person who is blind. Without sight, a person learns new ways to use the senses of touch and hearing. Blind people find ways to do almost everything.

Some blind people use Seeing Eye dogs to help them move around obstacles.

Vision Basics

People with normal sight have 20/20 vision. They can see at twenty feet what the average person sees at that distance. People with vision of 20/200 or less are legally blind. When people have 20/200 vision, they see at twenty feet what most people can see from two hundred feet away.

Most blind people have some sight. They may be able to see movement, color, or large objects. Some blind people can tell the difference between light and dark. Blind people may have trouble seeing if lighting is too bright or not bright enough. Their eyes may get tired faster, too. Blind people may be able to read large print, but find that their eyes get tired after the first few pages. About one of every ten blind people is totally blind. A totally blind person cannot see anything at all.

Many devices help people with low vision use the sight they have. Strong lenses called magnifiers make everything look larger. Computer programs can make the text and images larger on the screen.

Blind people face a variety of challenges. The world is set up for people who can see. Printed menus

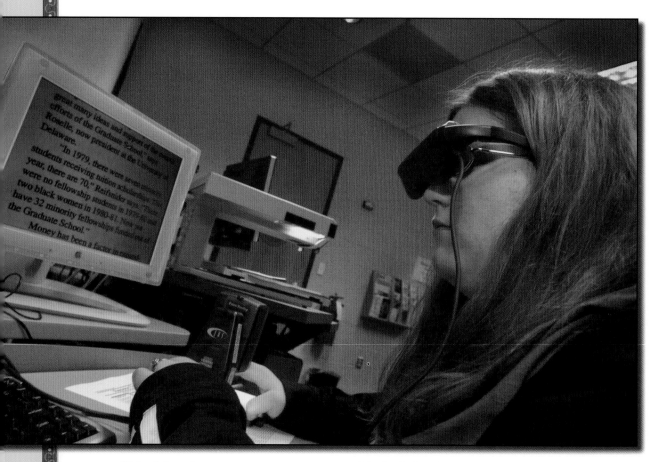

This girl reads text on a computer screen with the help of magnifying glasses. The glasses make everything bigger.

and street signs, computer graphics, and the labels on packages all are meant to be read by sight. Sight is needed for driving a car.

Despite these challenges, blind people find many ways to live full and busy lives. Although blind people cannot read print, they read Braille, listen to

Instead of using guide dogs, some blind people use miniature horses.
These horses are specially trained to help people get around during their day.

From Scanner to Speech

Blind people can use electronic scanners that turn print into computerized speech. Some scanners are the size of copying machines. Others are small enough to carry in a purse or backpack.

audiobooks, or use scanning technology. They travel using guide dogs or long white canes, and take trains or buses to get where they want to go.

Because sighted people may think blindness is scary, they have a hard time understanding how blind people live their lives. Sometimes sighted people think blind people are helpless. They try to keep blind people from doing things that they think will be hard or dangerous for them.

This man is reading a book with the help of a scanner. The scanner reads the text aloud so he can hear it.

Chapter 3

The Fun of Competition

Sometimes on spring days Alex Gamino stays after school to play beep baseball. Beep baseball is a form of the game made especially for blind players. The ball makes a beeping sound so the players know where it is. When a player hits the ball, the bases give a different beep. By following the sound, the players know where to run. Everyone who plays beep baseball must wear a blindfold. Blind and sighted players play as equals.

Alex is eight years old and in third grade. He lives in Illinois, with his parents and his older brother, Nick. Alex spends part of the school day in a resource room for blind children. The rest of the time he is in a classroom with kids who can see.

Alex Gamino loves to be outside playing games and visiting places like Joshua National Park.

In the resource room Alex learns to read and write Braille. He uses an abacus to do math problems. Later he will learn to use a computer with screen reading software. A screen reader is a program that reads aloud the words on the screen.

Alex has a bit of sight in one eye. He can read both Braille and large print. He is a very good Braille reader.

The Chicago Comets at practice. They are a visually impaired baseball team and play beep baseball.

Two years in a row he won prizes in the Braille Challenge. The Braille Challenge is a national contest. It tests reading, writing, and proofreading skills.

One of Alex's favorite hobbies is playing chess. He learned chess from his father, who is a serious player. On Alex's board the black squares are raised above the white squares. Each square has a small hole at the center. The chess pieces have pegs on the bottom that fit into the holes. When he studies the board, Alex can touch the pieces without moving them out of place.

A Little Math Help

The abacus is a device with beads that slide along thin metal rods. By sliding the beads up and down a person can add, subtract, multiply, and divide. The abacus is widely used in some Asian countries. Many blind people in the United States use the abacus because it allows them to do math without a pencil and paper.

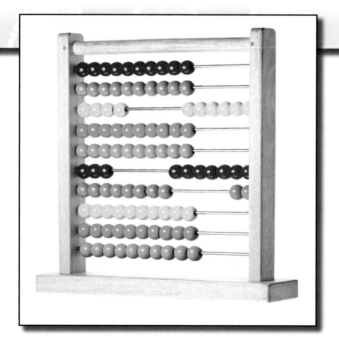

The Braille 'n Speak machine and abacus help this student during a math test.

Alex has a lot of ideas about what he'd like to do when he grows up. He thinks it would be fun to work in a store. It would be interesting to be a doctor, too, but he knows that would be hard work. His father tells him he has the brains to become a chess Grandmaster. Grandmasters are the best chess players in the world.

Alex loves to play chess. It's one of his favorite hobbies.

Chess boards for the visually impaired have the black squares raised higher than the white squares. This helps the players know where all the pieces are on the board.

"Being blind won't stop me from doing anything I want to do," Alex says. "I know blind people do all kinds of things. I can do whatever I want."

Chapter 4

New Homes in a New Land

Ai Yong was born in China. For several years she lived in a foster home, waiting to be adopted. In the city where she lived, blind children were not allowed to attend the local school. For three months Ai Yong went to a boarding school where blind children live. She was very unhappy there, and was glad when her foster mother brought her back home.

Ai Yong was adopted by a family from the United States when she was eight years old. Her new family added to her Chinese name. Today her full name is Ashleah Aiyong Chamberlain.

Ashleah Chamberlain was adopted at age eight.

Ashleah already knew a little bit of English when she came to the United States. She quickly mastered thousands of new English words and learned the Braille alphabet. Soon after her arrival she entered the nationwide Braille Readers Are Leaders Contest.

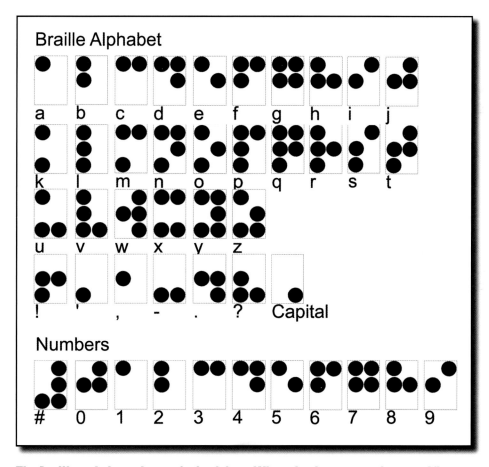

The Braille code is made up of raised dots. When the dots are put in a specific order, they represent letters and make it easy for visually impaired or blind people to read the text with their fingers.

She won the Jennifer Baker Award. This prize is given to a student who overcomes unusual challenges to learn Braille. Ashleah had become fluent in English and learned English Braille in only a few months!

When Ashleah went anywhere in China, she always held someone's hand. Things changed when she came to live with her new family. Ashleah's mother is a teacher of orientation and mobility (O & M). She teaches blind people to move around on their own by using a long white cane. Ashleah's mother gave her a cane and showed her how to use it. Soon Ashleah was walking by herself at school, at shopping malls, and in the park.

Not long ago Ashleah learned to crochet. She made a small blanket and sent it to her foster mother in China, whom she calls Aunt Elizabeth. Ashleah takes Chinese classes to help her remember the language. At a music program she sang "Are You Sleeping" in Chinese and English.

Like Ashleah, Rupa Sprecher was adopted from overseas. She spent her early years at a boarding

Ashleah loves to play in the park.

school for the blind in India. The school had about eighty-five pupils. Rupa slept in a room with seven other girls. Most of the children had families, but some, like Rupa, were orphans. There were very few Braille books or other supplies.

When Rupa was seven she was adopted by an American family. Her teachers and classmates gave her a big goodbye party. They were sad to see her leave, but happy that she was going to a loving home.

When she reached her home in Chicago, Rupa had to get used to many new things. Air-conditioning, refrigerators, showers, and TV were all surprises. She had to learn to use silverware and to eat strange new foods. She didn't like most American desserts, but she found that she loved popcorn.

Rupa's father is also blind. Her mother has low vision and is a teacher of blind children. Rupa goes to the school where her mother works. She spends half of the day in a resource room, or special classroom, for blind children. During the rest of the day she is in classes with children who can see.

Getting Around

Orientation and mobility is the science of teaching blind people to travel without help from others. Most blind people use the long white cane. By tapping the cane back and forth ahead of them, blind people can feel curbs, steps, poles, mailboxes, and other objects. They learn to cross the street by listening to the sounds of traffic.

This boy is using his cane to help him get through the hallways of his school.

Certain teachers are trained to teach their students to read and write Braille.

When Rupa goes out with her parents, she and her father both use their long white canes. Rupa loves to walk fast wherever she goes. Her father reminds her how to use her cane so that she can walk quickly and safely.

Some day Rupa would like to get a guide dog. Her family has a retired guide dog named Amos. Rupa loves dogs and thinks it would be fun to have one that is trained to help her travel by herself.

Ashleah and Rupa have good memories of their lives before they were adopted. Since they came to the United States they have learned the ways of a new land. They have discovered that blind people can work, travel, run a home, and raise children. They are learning that, given the opportunity, blind people can do almost anything.

Guide Dogs

A guide dog is trained to lead a blind person around objects in her way. The dog also points out doorways and stops at steps and curbs. The dog wears a harness with a stiff leather handle. By holding the handle, the blind person can follow the dog's movements. By law, guide dogs can go with their owners on buses, trains, and airplanes. They can enter restaurants, stores, theaters, and other public places. Most training programs require a blind person to be at least sixteen years old before getting a guide dog.

Seeing Eye dogs need special training in order to help people who are blind or visually impaired.

Ashleah practices her Braille using a stylus.

Chapter 5

Pointers From the Experts

In the summer of 2007, ten-year-old David Thomas attended a three-week camp for blind children. The camp was held at the Louisiana Center for the Blind in Ruston, Louisiana. Nearly all of the camp counselors were blind. The camp was run by blind people to teach blind kids the skills they need to be independent.

David was scared at first when he went to camp. He had some sight and at home he used it as much as he could. At camp all of the kids had to wear light blindfolds called sleepshades. They learned to eat

David Thomas plays the drums.

meals, go swimming, play games, and do everything else without sight. David soon learned to do things by using his senses of hearing and touch. In fact, using his new skills was easier than trying to count on his poor vision.

The next summer David went back to the camp in Ruston. This time he wasn't scared at all. He learned more about using a long white cane. He walked confidently by himself on the streets of Ruston. The camp counselors often told the kids about their lives as blind people. They described going to college, playing sports, and finding jobs. For David, it was exciting to learn from people who knew about blindness from the inside.

When David was in seventh grade he lost his remaining sight. He became totally blind. People sometimes ask him if it was hard to lose the bit of sight he had had all his life. "It really wasn't all that hard for me," he says. "I'd learned to do things under sleepshades, so I wasn't afraid. I talked a lot to my friends from camp. Some of them had been through it, too, and they were a big help."

On Top of the World

Blind people take part in all kinds of sports, from swimming and tandem cycling to track and field. They play basketball by putting a bell in the hoop so that it rings when they make a basket. Wrestling is a popular sport for blind athletes. In 2006, a blind man named Erik Weihenmayer climbed to the top of Mount Everest, the tallest mountain on earth.

Erik Weihenmayer climbed Mt. Everest in 2006.

David is getting ready to have some fun in a go-kart.

The counselors in Louisiana encouraged the campers to be adventurous. David welcomed that message. When he got a chance to go surfing, he couldn't wait to give it a try. The surfing instructor showed him how to position his body on the board. David could hear the waves coming. The louder the

This girl and her counselor play at a lake during summer camp.

roar, the bigger the wave! The instructor yelled for him to turn the board and start paddling. Off he went! "It was great!" he says. "I loved it!"

David is very good at using computers. Some day he would like to start a company to develop new technology for blind people. Right now blind people use screen reading programs and other special products that are quite expensive. David would like to find ways for blind people to use these things without having to spend a lot of extra money. He also would like to teach blind people to use technology. "Blind people have taught me so much," David says. "Some day it will be my turn to pass along the things I've learned."

Chapter 6

Looking Toward the Future

Some day MarChé Daughtry would like to learn to ride a horse. "I think maybe steering a horse would be a little bit like driving," she says. "It might give me the feeling of what driving a car is like."

The human mind is fascinating to MarChé. She loves to figure out how people think and why they act the way they do. She says she might want to be a psychologist when she grows up. She knows she isn't always patient when she listens to people. Patience is something she will have to learn.

Anthropology is another field that interests MarChé. An anthropologist studies human cultures. He or she learns about customs and beliefs in different parts of the world.

"I'm going to face some challenges in whatever I end up doing," MarChé says. "I'm a girl, I'm African American, and I'm blind. But when I decide what I really want to do, I'll find out how to get there. A lot of other people have gone before me and paved the way."

MarChé is ready to accomplish all her goals.

Words to Know

abacus—A device consisting of beads that slide on thin metal rods, sometimes used by blind people for doing math problems.

beep baseball—A form of baseball adapted for blind players, using a ball that makes a beeping sound.

Braille—A method of reading by touch that uses raised dots to form letters, numbers, and punctuation.

guide dog—A dog trained to help a blind person live and travel independently.

legally blind—Having vision of 20/200 or less.

light perception—The ability to tell light from darkness.

long white cane—A cane used by blind people to detect steps and obstacles.

orientation and mobility (O & M)—The science of teaching blind people to travel independently.

resource room—A classroom for teaching blind students within a public school.

scanner—A machine that scans printed text and reads it aloud in computerized speech.

screen reader—A computer program that reads the text on the screen aloud.

totally blind—Having no vision at all.

Learn More

Books

Alexander, Sally Hobart. *Do You Remember the Color Blue? and Other Questions Children Ask About Blindness.* New York: Viking, 2000.

Bender, Lionel. *Explaining Blindness.* London: Franklin Watts, 2009.

Edwards, Nicola. *My Friend Is Blind.* North Mankato, Minn.: Chrysalis Education, 2005.

Souder, Patricia. *A Different Way of Seeing: Youth with Visual Impairments and Blindness.* Broomall, Pa.: Mason Crest Publishers, 2008.

Web Sites

American Foundation for the Blind.

http://www.afb.org

Lighthouse International.

http://www.lighthouse.org

National Federation of the Blind.

http://www.nfb.org

Index